EXPRESSIONS
from a
Reflective
Soul

From empty feelings to new beginnings

KIMBERLEY M.L. STOKES

AuthorHouse™
1663 Liberty Drive
Bloomington, IN 47403
www.authorhouse.com
Phone: 1 (800) 839-8640

This book is printed on acid-free paper.

Interior Image Credit: Floyd Kerr and Ezra Stokes

ISBN: 978-1-7283-3686-2 (sc)
ISBN: 978-1-7283-3687-9 (e)

Library of Congress Control Number: 2019919584

Print information available on the last page.

Published by AuthorHouse 12/04/2019

authorHOUSE®

This book is dedicated to my supportive loving husband, sons, and parents.
Patience has been my virtue!

Acknowledgments

My husband, Ezra Lamond Stokes, you have been my inspiration, encouragement, support, and strength. I could not have done this without you!

To Isaiah and Jabari Stokes, my sons, I hope to raise and instill the same morals, values, and upbringing that my parents instilled in me. You are my everything!

Thanks to my parents, Floyd and Vivian Kerr. You are extraordinary, down-to-earth people; who have set an example for me since I was a young girl. The life you both showed me was nurturing and included a learning process that helped me develop into the woman I am today. Thank you for life!

I give special thanks to my Daddy (Floyd Kerr) for providing his tranquil and hypnotic artwork. A self-described "modern surrealist and hip-hop expressionist," who combines art, education, and sports in his daily life, he interprets nature and life in his work.

I give special thanks to my husband, Lamond Stokes, for providing his heartfelt and serene artwork. Lamond says his art starts in his mind, bleeds through his soul, and is then released through his idiosyncratic style and technique, he calls emotional expressionism.

Special acknowledgment to my family and friends: The Joneses, the Kerr's, the Paige's, and the Stokes's; Jacquie A., Angie B., Errin B., Blondette C., Hannatu H., Derek D., Dayne F., Deirdre B., Sherneta G., Arthur S., and Shelli S. for supporting me during the ups and downs, trial and tribulations, victories and losses in my personal life and/or professional career. You all played a part in my growth!

BIG shout out to my Sista, rodawg, my ride or die, Marilyn Pitchford, you always make me stand in my truth even when I don't want to hear it!

Yusuf and Samir Paige, thank you for being the brothers I never had. You kept me grounded!

Thank you to Norma and Larry Paige and Neil Jones for always being there for me whenever I needed a helping hand. I am proud to be able to call you my aunt and uncles.

Table of Contents

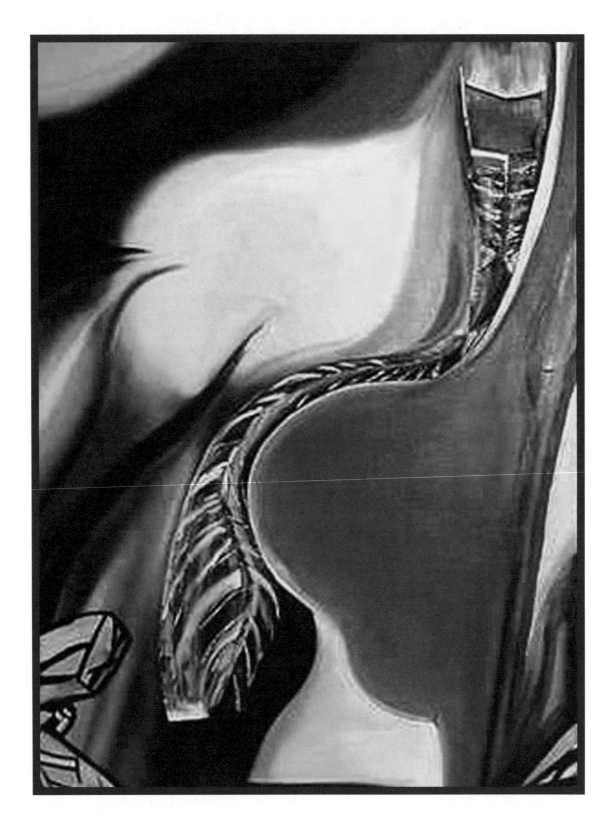

Expressions from a reflective soul

Over the years, I have been loved and have been blessed to love. Finding the right mate is difficult, but still I take chance after chance to find my "knight in shining armor," who will recognize my delicate nature and the pureness in my heart.

My strong king will compliment me and not set out to destroy me. My femininity, sexy, sassy Southern belle personality . . . there is one man out there who holds the key . . . to make my house a home. . .

Chapter 1
Empty Feeling

Overtime, one encounters love and hate, experiences heartache and misery, and has to deal with a myriad of emotions. These are life lessons leading to finding true love. Men and women share a common goal: the need to be surrounded by love. From adolescence to adulthood, we search and search for love, often finding instead the insecurities, vulnerabilities, and weakness we don't want to admit to. Maybe fear and/or denial cause us to ignore the snapshots presented to us of who we really are. It is important to remember that some of the guests we invite into our lives bring to the forefront some of things we don't want to see during the intricate moments experienced during our day-to-day lives.

Taking the time to revisit those snapshots will start your soul-searching process. This process is inevitable, regardless of your relationship status (in a relationship or seeking one). It is important to take the time to get to know yourself and what your wants, needs, and desires are. You will have to look at your current and past relationships to see if there is a pattern in the partners you choose. Look at the characteristics of your partners and determine what similarities they all have, both good and bad. Review them, study them, be honest with yourself, and you just might start to see a blueprint of the type of partners you choose to engage in a relationship with. Determine whether you contribute to the negative behavior that causes negative emotions. For example, if the men/women you date seem to take your kindness for granted, it could be because you reward your partner for both good and bad behavior.

It is important to remember that you are the only one who can change the type of relationships you encounter. So, determine the changes you need to make and begin the process of change from within. Love yourself, know yourself, trust yourself, continue to allow yourself to grow and be patient with yourself. In the end, all experiences and life lessons will guide you in finding the right partner.

A Soulful Cry

A heart torn
Feeling shame
Silent cries inside
Fallen weak to an emotion
Desperate for attention
Butterflies have flown away

That sparkle in my eye
That smile on my face
The laughter of happiness has been replaced
A soul lost in space
Drifting from place to place
Emotionless
Numb
As depression takes hold
Love has left me stranded on this deserted
highway
Hitchhiking in darkness
Please, Lord, take me away

Blinded by grief
Heart in hand
Raped by deception
As my mind tries to understand

Confused
Empty
Alone
On a never-ending road
No direction
Lost
Scared
With only the moon above
The pain so deep
One day this will be a memory
One day...
I will sleep

Do I want to die?
3
4
5 times I fantasize
Life without a soul
Is an empty place
Rivers of salt down my face

A face with no expression
A mind racing with aggression
A spirit of depression
A soul lost
Finding its way through deception
Masked by independence

Strength a mirage

Staying factual

Intelligence insurmountable

No support

No backbone

Slowly dying inside

Heart as good as gold

Good girl style...

Gave my heart, soul, and life to God

But the pain is so deep

I still fantasize

Death is not the answer

Reality strikes

Questioning all choices

As I fight for life

One breath at a time

Inhale exhale

The choices I've made

Why did I fail?

Classy sassy now a Southern belle

Sweet twang

Sunshine

The darkness has prevailed

Don't want to die

Live long

Stay strong

The words from Mother

I will live long

Grasping this concept

Getting out of this slump

I will not kill myself

My glory days are yet to come...

9

Liquid Pain

Mixed emotions

Misunderstood

In an endless sinking grave

Reaching for the skies while my hands are tied

Dropping fast in the pit of solitude

Make myself whole again

Look deep into my inner soul

What do you see?

A war between love and misery battling to keep me

What do you feel?

Sorrow? Pain?

Is this real... or

Is my mind playing tricks on me?

My emotions feel blame

Reality shows bad choices

I feel shame

Regain my dignity from this liquid pain

A Heart

A heart that has love is an overwhelming sensation of pure emotions

A heart looking for another is entrapped in an endless circle

A heart that found another is paired with the innocence of an angel and the passion of the devil

But

A heart like mine is smothered with pain and sorrow

Pain that makes you cry silent tears

And

Sorrow that makes you slowly die inside

A heart has

…love

…Joy

…Emotions

…And feelings

Why doesn't mine?

Trapped by an illusion

Living the life of a mistress
Love triangle
Both expecting
Home sweet home
Already have one bastard son
Trying to save face
Giving my son stability
Feel safe
Nine months later, another child in his place
Why am I making the same mistakes?
Gambling on life
He bluffed
It's my deal
Busted my deceiving lover who's not for real
Promise after promise
Trapped by an illusion of love
Caught in the manipulation of devotion
Heart guiding me through blinded emotions
Mind searching for a resolution
Love me or leave me
My time is about to end
Voices from the outside stressing my vulnerability
Too late gaining another responsibility
I am living by his words
I love you
Want you
Need you
Will be with you
My wife to be
The queen of this family tree
Repeating history
My mind prepared for flight
Vanish
I have my rights

To be free from all this animosity
Get my life together
Become a success on my own
Be independent and strong
No backbone
Caught up in the expression of my spirit
I will be 23
A youngster to this reality
Living day to day clouded by uncertainty
I'd rather believe in a dream than find a man of my own
A place to call home
Please, God, help me cleanse my soul
Negativity is seeping in this heart of gold
Giving all, I can to this man who is living two lives
Who keeps bamboozling me with his lies
Surrounded by his meaningless words
Sucked into a never-ending black hole
Walking through a blurred vision of reality
Transmutation and psychotic type of sanity
Two fathers with "self" on their conscious
No praise of fatherhood on their mind
I'm lost in a tornado of bad choices
Dragged through the slums of prostituting my soul for love
Started with a dream he would leave her to be with me
Why can't I move on from this fantasy?
Addicted to the drama this life brings me
I want to build a solid foundation for my two responsibilities
Ending in strength and the independence of my inner being
And...
Not an illusion of how I think it should be

Confused

My mind is skipping

My heart is bleeding

My eyes are blinded by liquid salt

My feelings shake from nervousness

Depression

Confusion

As animosity sinks in

Darkness surrounds every thought

Drowning in isolation

I wait for the moment

One second

One minute

One hour

My hour

For time to end

And

I awake from misery

…and shine once again

Tired

Drained

Empty

Sleepy

Confused

About what you mean to me

Comfortable

Relaxed

I try to be

I fall asleep

Deep

Deep

And then I dream

Why

My mind is racing
Where do I go? What do I do?
What is my purpose? How do i find you?
My heart slows to a standstill
Why! Why! Why!
Can't love find me?
Patience I have
A heart I have to give
Why! Why! Why!
Don't I feel fulfilled?
Is he the one?
Or just a fantasy?
Not reality
Realistically why would he want me?
Life goes on
Been here before
By yourself but not alone
No one to depend on
Why! Why! Why!
Is my life...
A blessing?
Or a curse?
The Almighty Divine tell me why? why? why?

Alone

Nowhere to go

No one to see

Feeling lonely inevitably

Meet people

Socialize

Over and over

Things stay the same

In the beginning

An adrenaline rush

Seeking

Friendship

    A companion

        A lover or... just lust?

The end is near

And the fear sets in

Starting all over again

Nowhere to go

No one to see

Feeling lonely inevitably

Losing Self

You left me

Lost in the shadows of the night

Alone again to face the world

In the midst of dawn

My heart has no feeling

My emotions

    Empty

    Numb

    Cold

Mind sharp as a knife

Bitter

I'm losing me

    Self

    I

    One

    Singular

No emotion

    Don't care

    Whatever

Soul Mate

Gone; left

Empty; alone

> A heart pumping with sorrow
>
> Look of serene expression on my face?

A mirrored image of what it once was

> Happiness; sunshine
>
> Your soul
>
> My soul
>
> Our essence together
>
> Connected by the universe
>
> Our love unfolds

A mirrored image of what it once was

> Shattered dreams
>
> Haunted memories
>
> Lies; deception
>
> The truth unspoken

A mirrored image of what it is now

> Ask the Lord, my savior, to bless me
>
> Fill my heart with joy
>
> Please, Lord, embrace me
>
> Destiny
>
> Fate
>
> I loved my Soul Mate

Gone; left

Empty; alone

I will wait patiently for my Soul Mate to come home

Why do I need you?

Why do I need you in my life?
I loved you
You hurt me
Why do I need you in my life?
You held me
Consoled me
Made me smile
I love you so deeply
Tears fall from my eyes
I need you
You complete me
Why does it hurt to say good-bye?
You used me
Deceived me
The pain I feel inside
My heart hurts
I'm lost
Confused
Feeling abused…emotionally
Gave you my sacred possession
You took
Have I learned my lesson yet?
Why do I need you in my life?
My heart has no feeling
No emotion
Lost in emptiness
A Red River flows
A heart with no joy
A drifter is how I feel
Drifting from place to place
No place to call home
My mind stops moving forward
My heart skips a beat
My love no longer exists
Who am I?
Amnesia
Lost
Don't know who I am anymore
You came and left so easily in one night
Future dreams shattered
Move on
Lost in the illusion of love
No emotions
A heart with no feeling I'm lost…
Lost in emptiness

Women's intuition

Something's not right
Can't put my finger on it
Felt this feeling before
Bad memories from the past
The outcome sucks
Scared of the certainty
Truth sets you free
But is free where you want to be?
Telling myself over and over again
God has a course set
Accept your chosen path
No real stability with love
Men come and go
How many times does a soul have to experience heartache before it dies?
Tired of all the lies
Giving your all
For what?
Why not put in the work necessary to make the relationship last?
At least it doesn't appear to be with me
Keep that third eye open
Understand God's plan
My mind
My mind
Losing self in myself
Searching for my inner soul
Feels cold
Distancing my goodness from evil
My heart
My heart
My heart
Beating to a foreign tune
What to do?
Scared of that intuition
Feeling consumed
Ask questions
Will I hear the truth?
Decipher the truth from lies
That intuition has taken over
Can't ignore your soul talking to you
Listen
Absorb
Make a crucial decision
Trust the intuition that keeps lingering through you

No Feeling

When you hate waking up in the morning

Heartache from the blues

So, upset you don't know what to do

Giving up on everything because you are tired of the bullshit

Breakdown

Fall to your knees

And plead

And plead

Lord rescue me

From this exhaustion and shame

From this anger and pain

I am numb with no feeling

Lost in reality

Wish for a fantasy

Trying to find my way home

Blocked by no feeling

Standing in the emptiness of my imagination

Charlatans

Keeping secrets

It's just a game

Two to three lovers

I am bouncing off the walls

An illusion of freedom in my mind

Bondage of intimacy that's a lie

Hostility is my karma

Arrogance is my mind frame

Everything is just a fantasy

My lies

My immaturity

To allow these indiscretions

Losing everything

Family

Kids

Love of my life

My wife

Self-respect

Cleanse my soul

On my way home

A love I once knew

I remember when I loved everything about you
Every pimple
Every Smiley
Every laugh
Every touch
Every word
Every scent
Every thought
Every dream
From head to toe
From how you wear your hats
To how you tied your hair in the back
From the sparkle in your eye when I said, "I love you"
To how mad you would get when I disappointed you.
How the word "baby" would fall off of your tongue and make me melt inside
Not sure what happened
Where did the feeling go?

WHY

WHAT'S WRONG WITH THE FANTASY OF UTOPIA

REDEEMING HOW YOUR LIFE IS SUPPOSED TO BE

WHY CAN'T YOUR HUSBAND NOT LIE?

WHY CAN'T YOUR PARTNER SUPPORT YOU AND GIVE YOU EVERYTHING YOU NEED?

WHY CAN'T THE SUNSHINE BRIGHT TO WARM YOUR HEART?

WHY CAN'T THE MOON CALM YOUR SOUL AND PREPARE YOU FOR WHAT YOU WILL ENCOUNTER THE NEXT DAY?

WHY CAN'T LOVE MAKE EVERYTHING BETTER?

WHY CAN'T A SONG MAKE YOU APPRECIATE ALL THAT YOU HAVE?

WHY CAN'T THE MEMORIES OF THE PAST BE PART OF WHO YOU ARE TODAY?

WHY CAN'T SELFLESS ACTS OF KINDNESS BE JUST THAT?

WHY CAN'T TEARS OF SORROW BE A CELEBRATION OF A LOVED ONE'S PASSAGE TO HEAVEN?

WHY CAN'T I JUST HAVE MY DREAMS BE GOALS I WORK TOWARDS?

WHY CAN'T I BE ACCEPTED FOR MY BRILLIANCE INSTEAD OF THE COLOR OF MY SKIN?

ALL THESE RANDOM THOUGHTS OF WHY

NEVER-ENDING QUESTIONS WITH NO ANSWERS

SO WHY ASK WHY

The Misguided

Delusions of freedom

Creates bondage

Immaturity

Not feeling worthy

Anger

Hostility

Sense of arrogance

Like cancer spreading through my body

Speak the truth on being freed

Selfish

Your side chick is a fantasy

She washes you off before you come home to me

Jealousy

Envious

Hatred for who you are

For what you have

Be your

Keep you

Inhibit your

Become you

Addiction in my mind

The flipside of me is you

Need to be you

Fulfill my failures

Lose my identity

Walk like you

Talk to you

Plot against you

In the end, I will erase you

Gone

No longer a threat

Don't feel better

Wasted a lifetime trying to become an image that really was not there

Gold Digger

Riches

Diamonds

Rent paid

Car upgrade

No time for love

No time for marriage

Will have a baby… more money… more money… more money

Greed

Self-pleasure

Fulfilling my needs

My wants

There is an "I" in selfish

No discrimination

Always seeking my next victim

On the prowl

Circling like a vulture around the high rollers

Sex kitten

Freak

Whatever you need

I can play any part in any scene

Keep me well maintenance

Never hear any complaints from me

Chapter 2:
Manifesting love, a new beginning

After misery takes its toll and the lifelong process of soul searching has begun, we are on a continuous journey of making our life lessons our strength. Being in love is an indescribable feeling. An emotion we need and cherish as human beings. Finding your soul mate is a blessing only from the Divine above. A blessing given to you ...a manifesting love ...your new beginning.

You should feel stronger and more confident. Believe me, it shows! Your confidence is evident and your positive aura glows. Pay attention to your surroundings. Observe the type of people you are attracting. Make sure they don't fit your old pattern. If they do, then drop them and move on. You don't need the heartache! Come on, we are not moving backwards. Stop the circle of those unsatisfying relationships. Remember what brought you here in the first place.

This healthier you is now sending out positive vibes to all you encounter. That higher frequency can only be heard and felt by those at the same or higher frequency. Confident in the type of partner you love, you have found a new experience. A new love! A love you didn't think existed. Please... please... please... enjoy each other with no pressure, no labels, and no boundaries. Just pure, unadulterated fun! We have manifested our soul mate to our own reality.

I present these reflections of love...

Me… You… Us… We – His and Her Essence

Childhood epiphany

       Growing up, I always knew

       The manifestation of my soul mate would come true

       Finding the one whose heart beats to the same tune

       Our souls napped on clouds and danced around the moon

       Silhouettes of our movements glisten like stars

       Two mystical beings

       Extremely modest with non-existing facades

Angels watching our enchanting bond

       God planned us for each other before we were even born

       Suddenly, we were blessed with a physical form

       Growing pains strengthened my psyche

       Life lessons inspired me to find my true love

Spirits getting stronger

       As we get closer and closer

       Our souls have shared devotion deeper than our physical being can display emotion

       Continuing to search for the passion my essence once knew

       Building our foundation until I find you

Immediately my spirit recognized you that day in August

       I stalled… Now our love is thicker than fog gets in fall

       Our souls' adoration reunited

       Destined for each other

       Found our way home

       Becoming husband and wife for eternity

       His and her essence has become one

Now that we are one

       We are a force to be reckoned with

       Two flexible personalities

       You're my palm

       I'm your fist

       Obstacles are merely an illusion

       Just a dramatic twist

       Of soul mates knowing love is bliss

Strength from my man

Strength from my man

Gives me the courage to succeed

Encourages my opportunities

Supports my dreams

Elevates my state of mind

He is truth

The positive flow of energy he releases to me

He is my protector

I can be me

Flaws and all

Emotionally linked to my soul

Mentally in sync with my mind

Physically inclined with my body

Shows me I can love someone all over again

My thoughts

    My words

        My actions

Speak

    Move

        Feel

Say his essence

King of my tribe

It is to hard describe the strength I receive from you

Your Smile

I love your smile

The way it brightens up a room

The twinkle in your eye when you are happy inside

No despair

No fear

Just exhilaration

The joy of being happy

Sun shining bright

No storms in the night

Comfortable

Enjoyable

Relaxed

Non-confrontational

Living life through a smile

Positive energy flowing around your aura

I am drawn to your smile

It brightens my life

Kindness surrounds you

Your smile affects everyone

So much grace

That smile

Your smile

Three words

Those three words
Emotional, physical, and mental
Living life through your heart
Feeling life through your touch
Understanding the philosophy of our love
Learning every nook and cranny of your human anatomy
Intellectually inclined to stimulate your mind

Those three words
Commitment, intimacy, and marriage
Bonding two hearts into one essence
Unity as one to build a foundation
An oath for eternal companionship
Matrimonial bliss

Those three words
Mind, body, and soul
Sacred connection
A Psychological blend of creativity
Feel your essence absorbing into mines
You're my reflection
When I speak your voice comes out of me

Those three words
I love you

A MANIFESTATION OF A SOUL MATE

Having your love is unbelievable

Incredible

Sensible

Pleasurable

Sanctified

Enjoyable

Memorable

Take this mind and make my love acceptable

Life lesson

Trusting the heart

Instead of fearing the unknown

Epiphany

A manifestation of a soul mate

Appease me

Relate to me

Enjoy me

As I summarize the joy I feel inside

You're my liaison between faith and fate

You liberate me

Free me

Rejuvenate me

Rehabilitate my soul

My love

My being as a woman

Finding a love so glorious

Destiny

Fate

Faith

The Divine from above you have chosen my path

He has given me a love I used to fear

I'm no longer alone

No longer fearing a fear from the past

My Test

You have brightened my thoughts

Whether I have you or not

Never felt so happy inside

Excitement

Feelings that lay dormant

Uplifted within

Fantasy of reality

My test of happiness

My test of time

Love is what I wait for

Your inner soul defines me

Your securities strengthen me

My test of pleasure

My test of time

Patience I'm blessed with

Whether I have you or not

I'm happy for the chance to feel emotions that lay dormant inside

My test is continuous

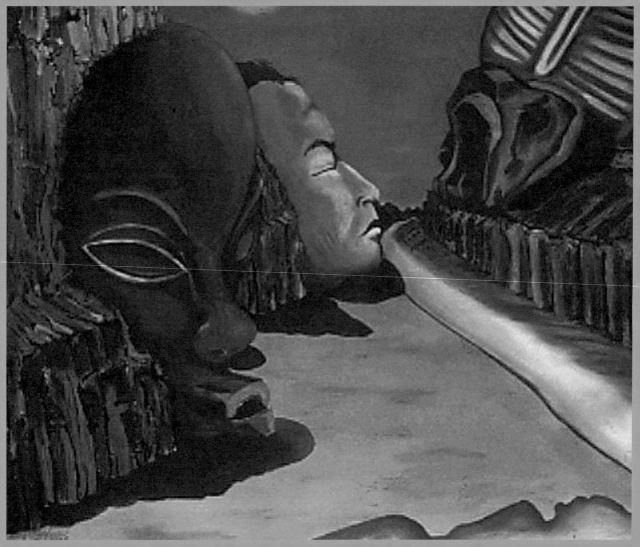

An everlasting journey

Commitment

An everlasting journey to happiness

As two hearts grow together

The souls become pure innocence

Destined for each other

Fate is inevitable

Separation is space with promiscuous temptations

Loving making is the force of two entities trying to unite as one

Honesty is the key to keeping trusting relationships

Minutes, seconds, days, months, years, decades, centuries

Our relationship will build, grow and strengthen

Our everlasting journey to happiness

Be Real

Stay honest with yourself

Believe with your heart

See with your mind

Feel for clarity

Happiness can be a reality

Law of Love

Love is the metaphor of continuity between two souls

Time is the space on which it exists

Intimacy is the bond of unity

Commitment is the law of relationships

A gentleman

You have shown me gentleness

A perfect sense of stability

My guard is up, fighting the battle between love and hate

Living in darkness

Will you be my light?

Take me away from the realms of twilight

My spirit is high

My love is pure

My sensuality is divine

It can be all yours

Pure passion

The ultimate pleasure of love… you will adore

Love that is deep… unique

Caressing the depths of your inner soul

Love can take you where you've never been before

Eager to understand my delicate nature

No limits

No boundaries

Waiting to see if you can bring out the best in me

And

If you succeed…I grant you ecstasy!

Touch of Innocence

You came in my time of need
A touch of innocence that caresses me

No expectations
You indulge me
Make me smile
Come hither

You dry me off
Keep me warm
Safe in your arms
As time darkens in the twilight
A silhouette of our essence dances in the moonlight

Your presence is strong
No more solitude
Laughter in the air
When you say "shorty" come here
A joy you bring
I want to share

No pressure
No boundaries
You allow me to be free
Every time you please me
I
She
Thee
My essence to be
You enjoy me

Mentally dedicated
What we share is not complicated
I enjoy your company, you keep me stimulated

Bad boy style with a touch of innocence
I get deeper than this
Does your essence have the patience?

Misbehaving

I Ain't Misbehaving

Wicked ...I am

Mischievous ...I Be

Naughty ...to the "T"

You energize me

Your essence surrounds my space

Spirit of truth

A soul to embrace

Enticed by the chase

Tantalize my mind

Mystified by these feelings for you inside

Ecstatic

Fascinated

Timid

Emotionally captivated

Sexually revolutionized by your presence

Desires awakened from unconsciousness

Solidify my passion

Open my Third Eye

The Art of Making Love

I Ain't Misbehaving

I just have this craving for YOU!

Wicked

As the clock strikes twelve

A devilish desire

An uncontrollable spirit

When will he unleash my sexual tendencies?

Pure and unadulterated

Love

Lust

Passion

Can he handle thee?

One man

Who shall it be?

The beast of sensuous pleasures takes over me

My sexuality roars, standing the test of time

A devilish passion

An uncontrollable desire

A man with sensuous pleasures will tame the wicked beast in thee...

Men

Men are…

The summer in winter…

And the…

Spring in fall…

When…

Two hearts are one…the LOVE IS INSURMOUNTABLE…

When…

Two hearts are two…the love is incompatible…

My summer…and…my spring

Never any darkness…my soul is complete…

I love you

I feel as if my time for love has come

I surrender

Used to feeling lonely with a heart filled with misery

Days filled with darkness

Then you came

Your warmth absorbs me from the coldness

My days are brighter

Wearing a smile, feeling your trusting warmth

Lonely nights driven away

Still seeking two hearts as one

As time passes, you will be me and I will be you

United as one

Mind, body, and soul waiting for the day

You say, "I Love You".

A love so deep

A love so deep
Deep into your emotions
Deep into your mind

Intensity
A soulful bond
Romantic bliss
A unique spirit
Your essence is divine
One heart...two souls
Exquisite beat
　　　...the rhythm of love

A love so deep
Deep into your emotions
Deep into your mind
You...
　　　Absorb me
　　　Become me
　　　Are me
　　　As our souls intertwine
You perspire my essence...you are part of me

See my heart through your eyes
Feel my heart through your touch
Sense my heart through your soul

As our love unfolds... A love so deep

Our love

Our love
Our love
I confess
When we first met, our souls already knew each other
With your first kiss, I knew you were the proclivity of love
You have given me an unconditional bond to your heart
The fantasy part of our love is over and the commitment to our love is here
Our love is not a destination but a voyage to a serene union

You are the bone from my ribs
God made you for me
We are one soul
When I see you smile
When I hold your hand while driving to nowhere
Night walks on the beaches of Savannah

You're my soul …mate
You're my heart …my courage
You're my love …my strength

All those years my homeys lied to me
Playalistic values kept me lonely
Finding your love has made me happy
Everyone keeps telling me
What we have is envied

You're my soul …mate
You're my heart …my courage
You're my love …my strength

My …my …my strength to love
My love
My soul

69

Test of Time

As the day ends

Missing you begins

As a newborn baby gets it first taste of life

I'm getting my taste of love

The first day out of 90

Love, faith, and happiness tested by the laws of nature

Questions that one might ask: Will he change?

Will change increase or decrease love?

Will I understand what I had when it has been taken?

Why does my heart feel torn?

Thinking like this from being in love.

Yes, love!

An uncontrollable feeling of happiness when you're near.

A feeling of desirable fantasy when you're away

No one can or will take your place

We share a love never felt before

An addiction

You are my high

The best thing in life is knowing you will always be with me mentally and physically

My test of time has come and I'm loving it

Because I'm loving you

50 years

When I said, "I Do"

Who would of knew 50 years later we are still so true

The Lord says we are two who become one flesh

Your body is mines

My body is yours

Respect for each other

Compromise

Love

Friendship

Giving everything, we have to this marriage

This life together

Celebrate this union

50 years later and our love is stronger than ever

Chapter 3
A Father's Love

There is no love greater love than that of a parent for a child. The love of mothers and fathers for their children is strong enough to withstand the most difficult of life's challenges. However, this love is sometimes exploited and used as a manipulative device when the parent's relationship begins to die. Unfortunately, women seem to be the wielders of this type of power more frequently than men; maybe due to the high percentage of women raising children alone. Too often, good fathers are denied the basic rights of fatherhood and the children are used as punishment, creating a no-win situation. Everyone suffers in such a situation: the father because he is unable to see his children and be a part of their lives; the children because they miss out on the experience of having a relationship with their father; and the mother because eventually the children will be old enough to speak their mind.

There are too many fathers who are deadbeats, abusive, no good, don't acknowledge their children, and/or who don't want anything to do with their offspring. The mothers of such children pray for any attention, support, or assistance they can get for their children from the fathers. It is difficult for most to understand why a woman would deny a father who wants to jointly raise their kids, love their kids, and support their kids. I am talking about the ones who are doing right …you know the positive and strong fathers!

The Reflective Soul Message:
Wake up, mothers!
A father's bond with his children has nothing to do with you! Girlfriend get over it and move on. It is amazing the number of women who have moved on, gotten married, and two, three, four kids later are still giving the first child's father hell. Is the unnecessary drama occurring because your life is not together? Is he to blame for everything bad that happens in your life? Think about it…does that make sense? We each have to accept responsibility for our actions and reactions recognizing that negative behaviors result in negative outcomes (often referred to as bad karma). You cannot expect to do wrong to people without bad things coming to you threefold. Good things happen to good people. God warned us not to mess with his anointed! That means the children. Remember, they are God's anointed.

I commend all parents who put their differences aside for the sake of the children. You know… the parents who work together to make their kids lives prosperous and joyful; parents who provide their kids with love and support, together, even when they don't live together.

Dear Daddy,
When are you coming to visit us? Mommy said you don't love us anymore. Daddy why did you hurt mommy heart? We miss you and love you!

Love
Sarah and Mommy

For those fathers who are good, loving and supportive of their children but are not able to see, speak or be apart of their lives; I feel your pain and I have to describe your emotions.

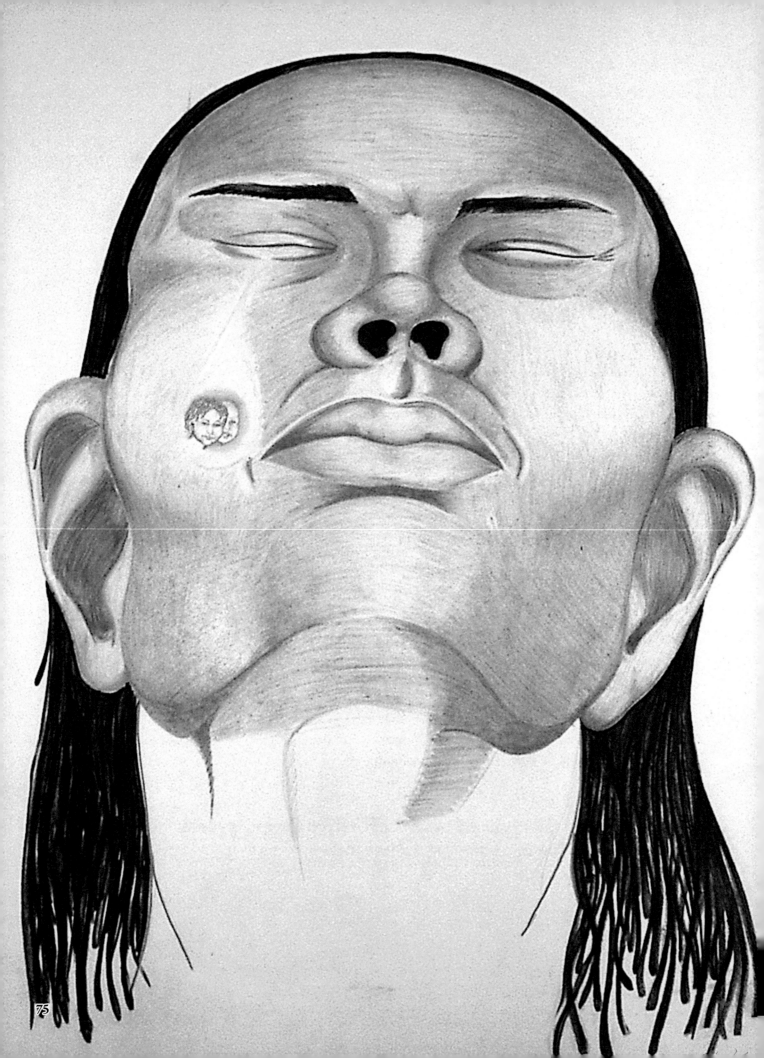

Fatherhood

Solitude

Feeling destitute

Deep thoughts in my mind

Wasting time

Quick fix – Get rich

Lonely for your voice

Emptiness only you can replace

Mind-shattering confusion

Blinded by darkness

Falling

Spinning

Spiraling

Can't calm down

Heart racing

Night sweats

Meditate

Hours

Days

Wake up

Still feel the same

Claustrophobic by these emotions of shame

My temple invaded

Discouragement

A thief in the night robbing me of my integrity

Frustrated male ego deprived of fatherhood

Agony clouds my judgment

Resuscitate my confidence as I cry inside

Distorted visions of our bond

Like a chameleon, I protect my inner emotions and camouflage my outer being

6-foot 3 inch; 170-pound mask hiding a hideous soul

The reasons for all this misery I'm just missing my BABIES!

Fatherhood Part II

My head

Struggling with the fact you are not next to me

Not focused

Stressed out

Telepathic tendencies

You have my devotion

My mind in motion

Clairvoyance

A father's intuition

Anything to have you close to me

Visualize about us at the park

Your hand in mine

On cloud nine

Your essence

Your presence

Your innocence

Massage my heart

Stroke my ego

Caress my pride

Angels given to me from the heavenly skies

Deep in thought

Losing my mind

My dreams

My reality

Unconsciously sabotaging my destiny

Visions of us preoccupy the psychosomatic jaded mind

Migraines every day

Missing you keeps me in pain

My heart

Thumps to an unfamiliar beat

Could it be arrhythmia?

The agony I endure from your absence

Feels like having a hollow point bullet pierce my heart

continuously

I'm half dead

As I tread through this sea of emotions

Pleading with the coldness of Medusa

The repercussions are conclusive

Fighting to stay alive

Fading to dust

No trust

Dramatized

Emotionally traumatized

I will strategize to have you in my life

My body

Fatigue

Malnutrition

No energy

Building up my strength to engage in battle

Holding onto what you mean to me

Suffocation from the enemy

Withdrawn from society

Losing my creativity

Sucked into a bottomless pit

Weakened by gravity

They are the proclivity of an unconditional love

Our visits together are short-lived

Time denied I couldn't get back

Lost memoirs

Why doesn't anyone understand that?

Set a foundation

Follow my path

Planted roots from my tree

My DNA

My genes

A girl and a boy

GOD has given me that I can't see!

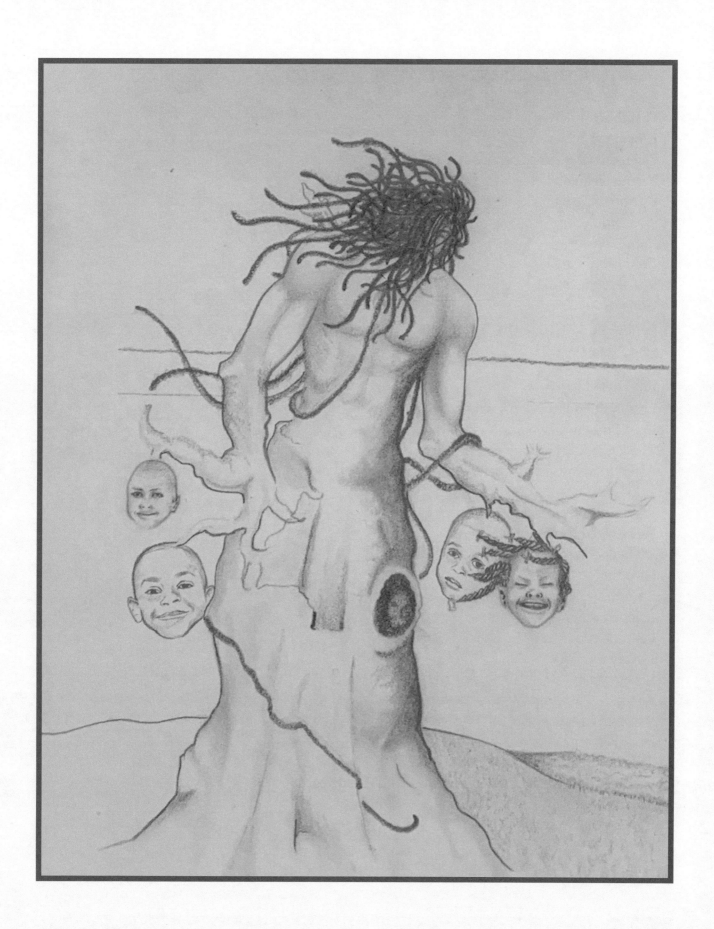

My subconscious

Past times
Hiding the misfortune
Hunted by my subconscious
Taking life in stride
Dishonest
No word
Adoration lost
Confusion
Where do I stand?
Gone astray
Misplaced
Dreams don't exist
Ambition strong
Where do I belong?
Lost in the misery of my subconscious
Can't find my way home
Challenged by life's metamorphosis
Adapt to many environments
Good, bad, truth, lies
Wanting to understand my meaning
Tears bleed heavily on the inside
Drowning in the obstacles of a dream
Help me
Save me
Reincarnate me
I am the most real
I will find myself
Lose myself
And
Recreate myself again
Hunted by my subconscious
Talking to a memory of my soul
Gathering my manhood like a puzzle with lost pieces
Put together with empty spaces
Finding my meaning
Being part of this world
Finding my purpose for existing in my own reality

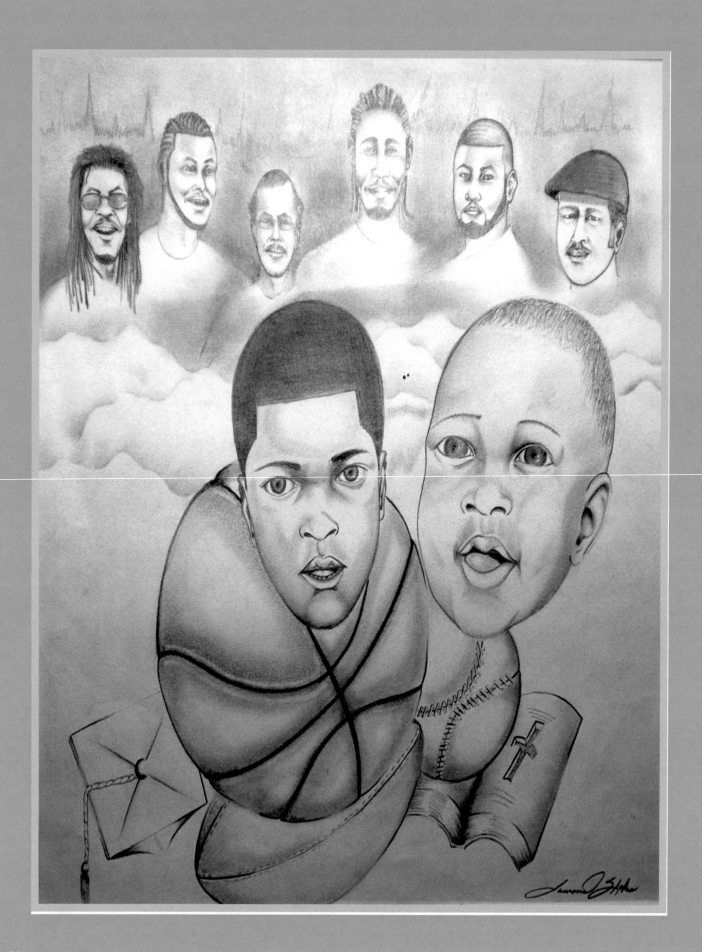

U

U support me

U teach me

U inspire me

U make me smile

U encourage me

U believe n me

U punish me

U lose 2 me

U keep me positive when things seem negative

U spoil me with what I need

U understand me

U listen 2 me

U talk 2 me

U nurture me

U love me

U like me

U are my inspiration

U tell me no

Daddy, you keep it real!

U are a blessing!

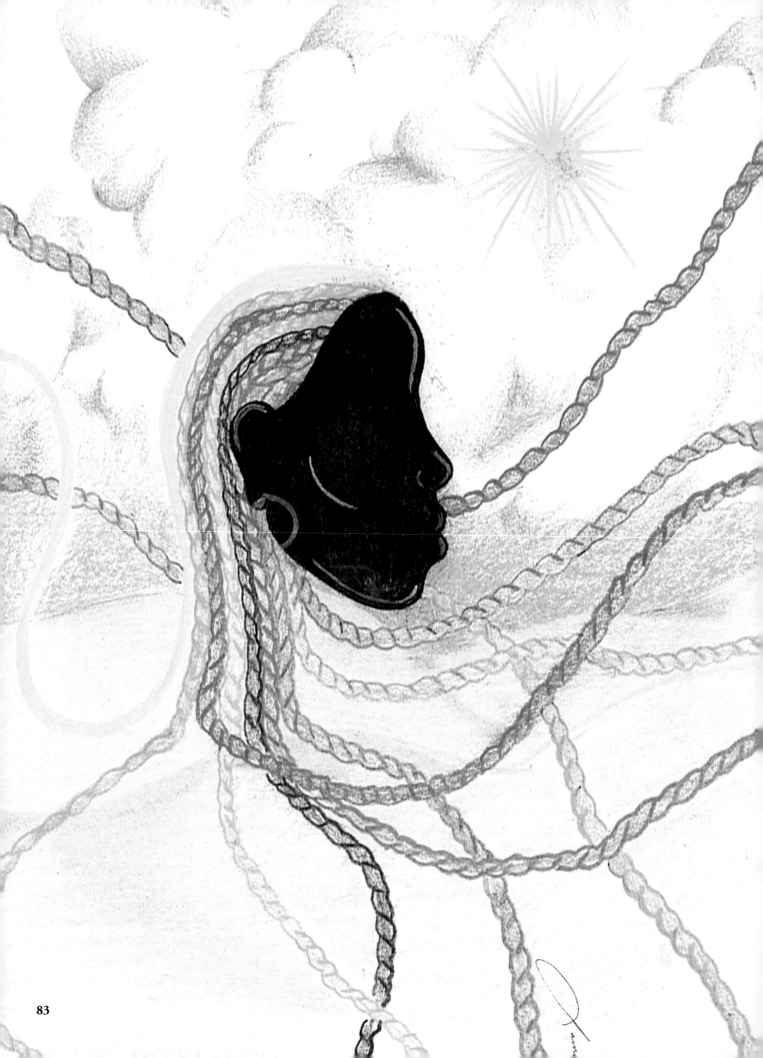

Oblivion

5-year-old little girl
Perplexed
Petrified of the hall's roar
Screams of desperation outside my door
Mommy busted by Daddy's friends
Get out
No love lost
We don't need you
Mommy no longer loves Daddy
He is gone in the wind
Who is going to read me stories and play with me 'til noon?
Mommy cries every night, blaming Daddy
Singing the blues
Lost in oblivion
Looking in the mirror
Now sixteen years old
Promiscuous straight "A" student
Trying to keep love close
Labeled a statutory rape victim
Father figures are all I see
This one
Or that one
Is all I need
No respect for authority
I don't understand why Mommy won't let me see Daddy
Lost in oblivion
2:30 AM
Wake up 23
With two irritating offspring bothering me
Deja Vu
Walking in Mother's footsteps
Kicked Daddy to the curb
Don't need him
Can't stand him
Moving on to someone else
Filled with anger and hate
Blaming everyone else
For mistakes made
Don't even remember when this all started happening
Lost in oblivion
Life of resentment
Emptiness
No pride
Now, I remember when I was five
Mommy left Daddy... cut all family ties

Not being able to see my father has created this monster inside

Malicious

I can't get over your absence
I feel incomplete without you
The only way to make you hurt is to keep the kids from you
Love has evaporated
Comfort has set in
We were a routine that suddenly had to end
Scared to move on
Confused about whom to see
If we stayed together
Not sure if I would have been happy
My malicious ways
Often, I want to apologize for what I have put you through
Pride puts me in a headlock
I can't move
Ego has me chained down in this inner dungeon of mine
Every time I'm ready to give in
I break down and cry
Darkness has prevailed
I don't know why
It seems easier to hate you
Vicious state of mind
My malicious ways
One moment in time
I will no longer deny the pain I have caused inside
Wasted all of this time on negative energy
Plotting and scheming
Don't know what got into me
Now it is all optimistic
Grant your serenity
Gained my sanity
Giving my soul to the Holy Trinity
Leaving my malicious ways behind

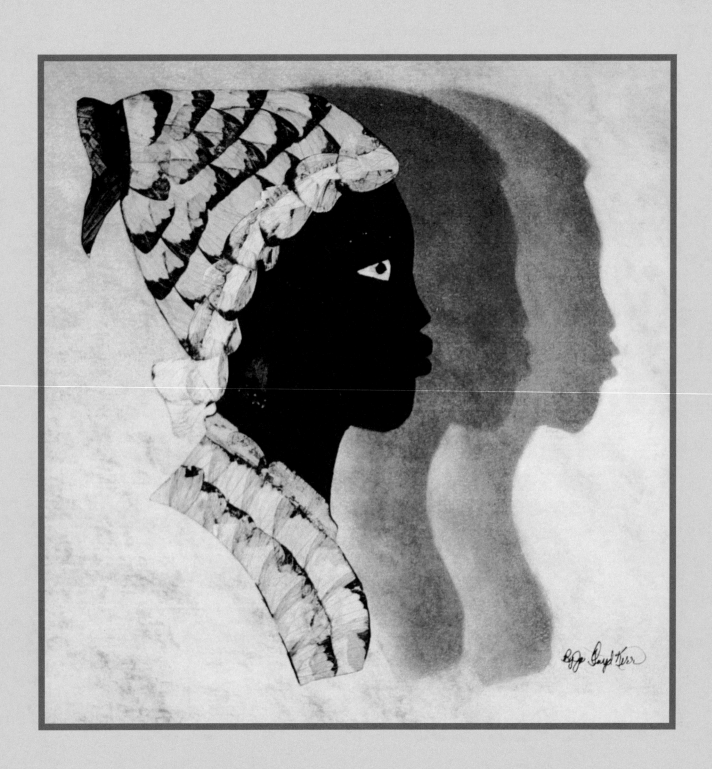

Pregnant attitudes

<u>15 years old</u>
Pregnant
Not finished with school
What do I do?
Who can tell?
No job
No life
Taboo
Father young too

<u>25 years old</u>
Pregnant
Fresh out of college
Starting my career
Foundation being made
Am I ready to be a parent
Wow we are just dating

<u>35 years old</u>
Pregnant
Established in my life
Stable
Soon to be a wife
I know what I want
Foundation is made
Looking forward to motherhood

<u>45 years old</u>
Pregnant
Have I lost my mind?
Just starting to really live my life
Top of my game
Thought I was going through menopause
Children all grown
20-year anniversary
Expecting a newborn

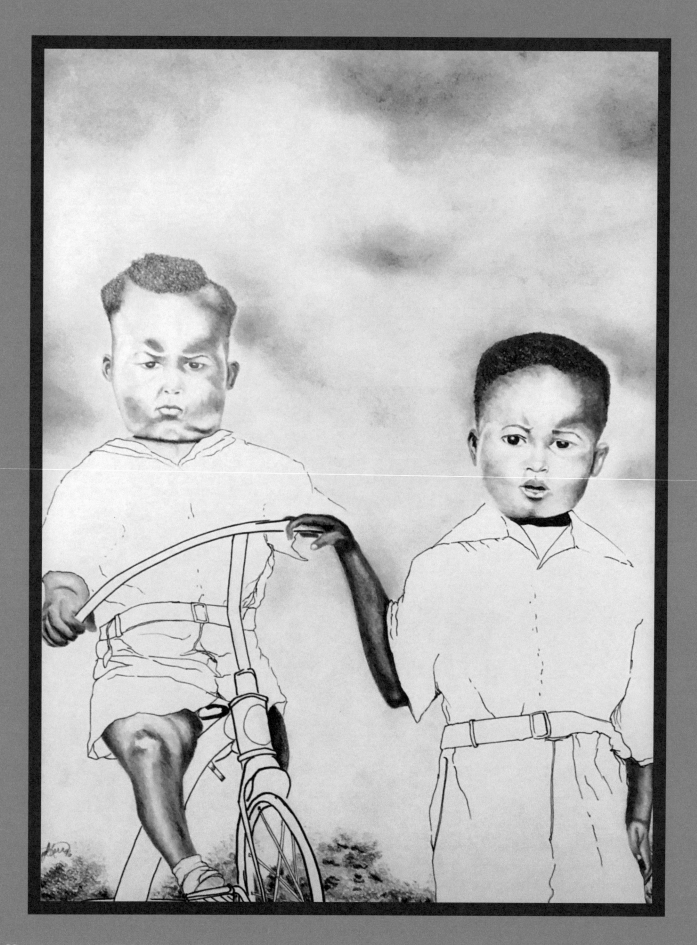

Offspring

I never felt a love like this

My sons whom I adore

You bring out the you in me

The innocence in your eyes

Curiosity in your smile

I will teach you to develop your Chi

My prince

True royalty

Part of my life's meaning

I hope to pass on my legacy from generation to generation

Remember the past to change the future

My lineage

Chapter 4
Trials and Tribulations

Sometimes we as people do not realize how our everyday experiences stress our souls and change our happy spirit. Life is what we make it. Society cannot dictate your life unless you let it. We have trials and tribulations every day and we will conquer them one step at a time. Obstacles are not always what they seem to be.

This chapter will have you questioning some of your answers instead of looking for answers to all of your questions. Everything is everything!

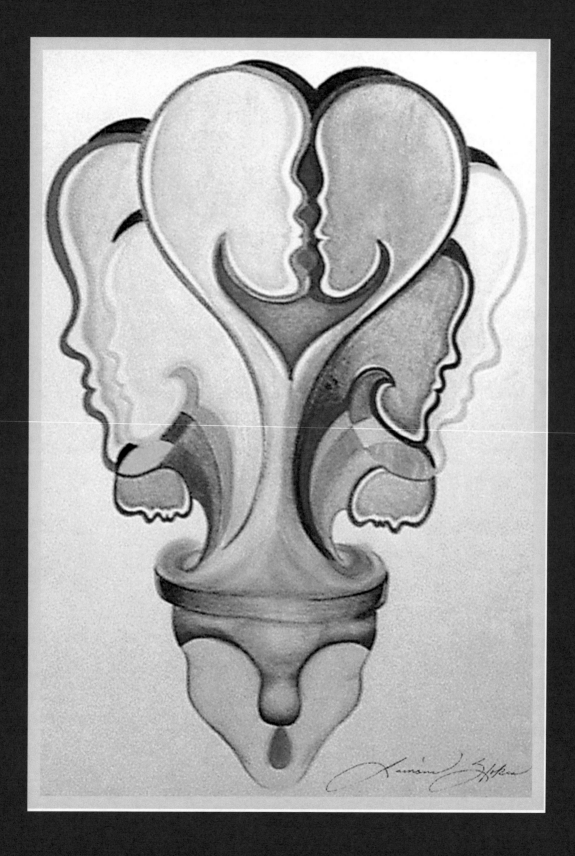

STRONG PERSONALITY

REACTING WITHOUT THINKING

BELITTLING COMMENTS ARE SAID

YOU'RE WOMEN IN A HIGH POSITION

LETTING STATUS GO TO YOUR HEAD

WE ARE NOT BENEATH YOU

CORRECTING OUR EVERY MOVE

YOU ARE HYPOCRITICAL

UNETHICAL

STEREOTYPICAL

MANIPULATIVE

VINDICTIVE

STRINGENT

DISRESPECTFUL

WITH A PROBLEMATIC ATTITUDE

STRONG PERSONALITY?

NO, JUST RUDE

TACTLESS

CALLOUS

NO CULPABILITY

NEVER YOUR FAULT

WANT FOLLOWERS?

BE A LEADER

NOT A SLAVE MASTER

SARCASTIC COMMENTS

WHERE IS YOUR INTEGRITY?

COME DOWN OFF YOUR HIGH HORSE

EARN OUR RESPECT

STRONG PERSONALITY SHOULD BE YOUR PRESENCE AND NOT BY WHAT IS SAID

SHARE YOUR WISDOM

SPEAK FAIRNESS

LIVE BY HONESTY

REVEAL STRENGTH IN YOUR CHARACTER

TO SUCCEED

94

Woman's Worth

No kids
No husband
They say "a woman's worth"
Failing
Ostracized
Diseased
Society keeps asking what's wrong with me
Look at my reflection what do I see
An incomplete woman taunting me
Failure in love
Or
Success in my dreams
Which part of my life is not reality?
I know God's not punishing me
Having your own family to love and protect
A gift from God I will cherish and respect
This gift I have not received just yet
Am I wishing upon a distant star?
Do I have a misunderstanding of woman's worth?
Or
Is the misunderstanding the norm of an American dream?
Societal pressures keep me depressed and inhibited
Family innuendoes make me want to cry
Waiting until marriage feels like a vision instead of a possibility
I guess in actuality
Society's mentality
My reality is...
I don't need a husband or my own kids to feel a woman's worth
Just a man and some kids who will love me for me

American Dream

The American Dream
Is it for me?
A Black woman
Struggling to be accepted
Bow down to hypocrisy
White dream laughs at me
Black man, please support me
Challenged by patriotism
Lost in a web of superiority
Whiplash from racism
Misguided by fantasy
The American Dream
Suffering from post-traumatic:
      Racism
      Stereotypes
      Bigotry
      Chauvinism
      Inferiority
A Black woman
Confined to laws that don't protect me
Which House of Representatives represents me?
This maze of life
Who am I supposed to be in this American Dream?
Strength put upon me
Independence taught to me
Struggles have shown me
Poverty accepting to me
Is the American Dream meant for me?
Trapped in American's wasteland through desperate measures
I hear the bells of freedom ring
Am I at peace?
Or am I at ease?
White dream, please let me be
History embedded in my mind
Pain rooted in my heart
Visions implanted in my eyes
How can I have an American Dream that's not meant for me?

Mirror Image

10-year-old girl trapped in a mirror image
Reflection of being true
True
An imperfect word
Distressed by my subconscious
Causes pain to the spirit
10-year-old girl suppressed inside
Go back and hide
Truth become lies
Why are you trying to conceal the feelings inside?
Break down and silently cry
Chasing a lifeless body surrounded by agony
Memories play hide-n-seek
A game I have to play
She is not a child anymore
Damaged goods
A child to a woman in one single night
Loss of pure innocence
Mirror image
Back to the realm of my subconscious
Revealing my true being
Being
An impersonal word
Reverse my reflection
She stares right back at me
Mirror image
What does she see?
A 10-year-old sensitive she-devil haunting me
Or
Thirty-year-old women mystified by nostalgia
Cogitation of the inner soul
Stand strong and never sigh
Lies becomes truth because you…
Alter your mind
Hide your heart
Change your being
Lose your identity
Lost in a mirror image of my own reflection

My Mother

You set my foundation

Your strength... Protected me

Your knowledge... Mentored me

Your courage... Supported me

Your happiness... Fulfills me

My mother... An exceptional woman

Your faith... Gave me spirituality

Your love... Believes in me

Your success... Encourages me

Your presence... Secures me

My mother... An extraordinary woman

Your guidance... Raised me

Your heart... Believes in me

Your soul... Is my essence

Your struggles... Teach me

My mother... A remarkable woman

A strong black queen

A motivator

You are my inspiration

My mother... A phenomenal woman

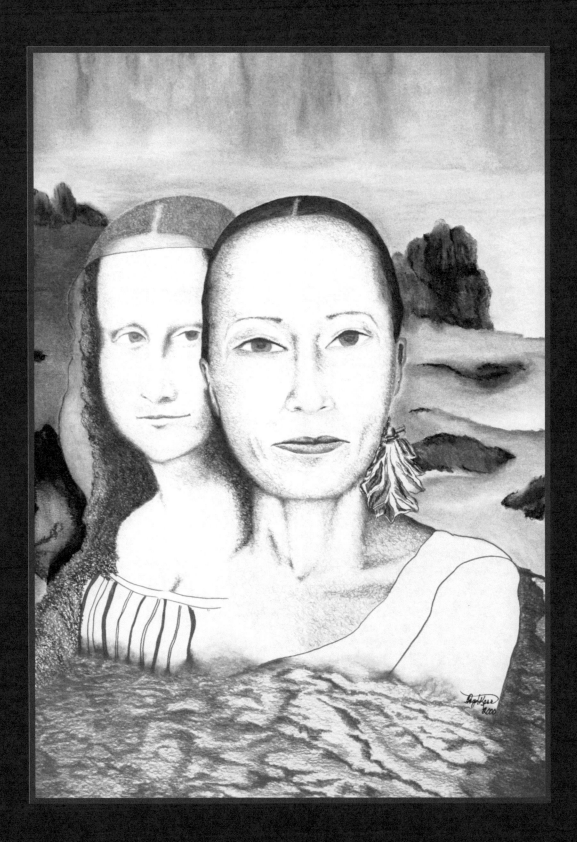

Black and White

Political prisoner of cultural diversity

Forced to live amongst the unknown

A life to live not chosen by me

Moved from the world I knew

The voice inside

My heart's cries

As the storm of gunfire fills the skies

Will my kids and I survive?

Who am I?

No religion

No race

Just a being

A life without choice

My mind is torn

Dictatorship

Freedom

Democracy

Freedom

Let me live the life God meant for me

Who am I?

Not free to express my mind

Can't make money anytime

Hear my voice

Soar

Fly high

Independence

Who am I?

Peace of mind

It's not written in black and white to define

my being

Look upon my eyes

See me for what I am to be

Watch me lose my identity

Hear me cry for praise

Feel my pain

The strength in my presence

The struggle in my speech

Study my character

Welcome my affirmation

A peaceful karma

Who am I?

A Being

Empowering my mind, body, and soul

Uniting my sisterhood

Who am I?

The backbone to all societies

The nurturing force to all families

The protector of all offspring

The queen of all tribes

We fight for humanity

Who am I?

A refugee

Rebirth

Fighting this feeling inside

What to do, I can no longer hide

This shell

My cocoon

Protects me

Safe inside

A metamorphosis

Like a butterfly

What will happen when I come outside?

Four more months

And the process will begin

30 years old

A rebirth from within

29 years of molding and self-searching

29 years

I know who I am

Layer by layer

As the shell cracks and breaks

Layer by layer

As this change will take

Time passes on

Sometime in May

Will be the day

Time stops for no one

Not even on my 30th birthday

What I See

Dedicated

Strong

Intellectually inclined

The proclivity of a business mind

Today is your day

Your rebirth has taken place over time

Are 40-something

Look 30-something

As your aura shines

Stay witty

Gain wisdom

All life lessons give freedom to your mind

As you grow older

Your metamorphosis

I see a compassionate silhouette of your inner being on the outside

Keep love, hope, and faith close to your heart

I wish you peace, blessings, and happiness

Happy Birthday

This is what I saw from the start!

Camouflage

I trusted your guidance

All that Holy talk

Until one day you felt threatened

Your true colors were camouflaged

Envy and jealousy seized your soul

You bamboozled me

Had me questioning

What did I do wrong?

Striving to be in the spotlight

Stepping on toes to get ahead

All over territorial power trips

Looking for underlying motives

I laughed and shook my head

I ask GOD every day to look out for you

You know not what you do

For some reason acknowledging your pettiness

Is reality unknown to you?

Being iniquitous to honest people

Disrespect is no respect

I trusted you

Non-communicative

Don't want to be bothered

Your insecurities are exposed

Disposition amuck

Second guessing

Undercutting

Snide remarks

Hypocritical

I am sad to say

The truth spoken come judgment day

You misinterpreted my temperament

I will never let you in

You only get one opportunity to be my friend

You are not a friend nor foe

Just a "Being" who takes up space

I know we are all only human

Mistakes will be made

Just remember, those of you out there claiming to be saved

Periodically look at your own reflection

Changes may need to be made

Delivered from evil; Katrina's wrath

And then came Wind
And then came Water
       Global warming
       Revelations
       Praise him
       Understand his notice
       A propensity to take life for granted
And then came Flooding
And then came Disaster
       Devastation from ignorance
       A test of devotion
       Repent your sins
       Ask for absolution
       Our salvation
And then came Displacement
And then came Disease
       Good vs. Evil
       Deprivation
       Mystification
       Figment of your imagination
       Pandemonium
       No equilibrium
       Best of the best … worst of the worst
       Lives shattered by Katrina's wrath
       Cleanse your soul in a spiritual bath
And then came Riots
And then came Death
       Catastrophic pain
       Armageddon
       Satan's deceit
       Souls lost forever
       The devil's playground
       Demon soul catchers on the rebound
And then came Darkness
And then came Light
       Evil trickery strives to betray you
       Take heed of the Devil's mirage
       Rebuke evil's camouflage
       Depend on the Divine to guide you through the night
And then came Hope
And then came Faith
       Believe in him
       Enter his Kingdom
       Be reborn
       He came
       And
       Delivered us from evil
And then came a New Beginning

HOMELESS

NOWHERE TO GO

DARK MIST WHISK ACROSS MY FACE

KEEPING SILENT

BLENDING INTO THE NIGHT

USE DRUGS AND ALCOHOL TO GET ME THROUGH 'TIL DAWN

MENTAL INSTABILITY

WALKING AROUND THESE COOL WET STREETS

STOMACH PAINS MAKING ME DIG IN GARBAGE

SPOILED ROTTEN FOOD BUT I'M FULL

BEG FOR MONEY NO LUCK

WHEN WILL I PREVAIL

I WAS SOMEBODY BEFORE KATRINA AND THE LEVEES FAILED

TRYING TO SURVIVE TO STAY ALIVE IN THIS CUT-THROAT WORLD

RECEIVING BLESSINGS EVERY NOW AND THEN

WHY DID I TAKE LIFE FOR GRANTED?

LORD HELP ME FIND MY WAY

CLASSIC WORDS TO SAY

REDEMPTION

STREETS PERCEPTION

CONSTANT REPETITION

LOST IN THIS WEB OF PANDEMONIUM

WHO OPENED PANDORA'S BOX?

AM I …ARE WE ALL WILLING TO SACRIFICE

THOUSANDS OF US WITH NO PLACE TO CALL HOME

STRUGGLING TO UNDERSTAND PURGATORY

NOTHING BUT DISTRESS

HAVE I SUCCUMBED TO IMAGINARY HELPLESSNESS?

I WAS SOMEBODY BEFORE THIS

OVERCOMING DARKNESS

Worries consume us

Fear paralyzes us

Anxieties tear us from our confidence

Powerless

Afraid to dream

Obsessed by worries

Consumed by darkness and self-doubt

Feeling inadequate

Overcoming darkness

Manifest from within

Liberated from our fear

Pretending you have courage

Self-love

Convinced yourself fear is conquered

Break the shell

Tricked myself into bravery

Overcame the emptiness of self-defeat

My Third Eye

His mediation
His affirmation
His visualization
Energetically stimulate
Remove these blockages from my being
Uninhibited free-flowing energy
My vibration has made a difference in my vitality and resilience
My transformation
Alchemist spirit
I am seeing my inner self
I am intuition
I am one with my higher self
I AM
I AM
I AM

Broken down

Tired
Exhausted
Ready to give up
or
stand in the moment?
Did I really say I do to you?
Manipulation
Lies to justify
No savings
No money
No life
No conversation
Am I self-married?
Constant criticism
Taken for grated
Selfish
Broken down
Amnesia
Who am I?
Why can't I remember?

Sucked into a life of nobody
Draining to the last perspiration drop
Mentally you beat me down until I have Amnesia
Emotionally you manipulate my delicate humble nature
Physically you see my body lose shape and flexibility
No blame
Just shame
Recognize your part in this lifeless silhouette
Shut down
Maybe a nervous breakdown
Sometimes I wonder if my heart stops will anyone notice
No longer fight for what is right
Broken down to emotionless
Mind weakened by your mendacities
Nothing left
Gave my life to the Lord
He heals the soul and combat wounds
He feeds me inspiration
Removed desperations
No longer fearful, sad, and insecure

Wrath	Envy	Greed
Rage	Resentment	Rapacious
Vengeance	Why are you happy?	All for the taking
Uncontrollable anger	Good life	My share and yours
Feel my wrath	Good wife	Money
My aftermath	Promotion after promotion	Cars
Like a psychopath	Moving up at work where	Women
Ascension	I want to be	All things attractive
Leveled dimensions	No worries	I will take it all
Negativity feels the air	Lots of money	Give me
Tension flares	Why not me?	No reciprocation
Temples pulsating to a	Loving parents	TKO anyone in your way
jagged serrated tune	Nice neighborhood	Find in your heart a change
Blood flowing like lava	It should be me!	in tune
Ready to erupt	Don't understand all the	Generosity
Rage targeted towards the	good things you receive	No longer feeling blue
ones you love	My desires are your	Giving
Heat-seeking missile out to	possessions	Sharing
destroy	If I can't become you, then	Helping
Have patience over anger	destroy you	Guiding others to be
before you die alone	I am that crab in the bucket	generous over greed
	holding your toe	
	Rid these feelings of envy	
	I embrace kindness this	
	virtue of mine	

MY BLACKNESS

Talk proper
Raised in the suburbs
Not the Eastside
Owned home
Not in the projects

Why do you question my blackness?
No hood
No drugs
Not a thug or banger
Not a killa
Do love my scrilla

Don't question my blackness!
Learned my enemy
Adjusted to white America
The "Art of War" conquer and take over
Strategized wealth and success
Educated
Independent
Legitimate hustler
Set foundation
Make money
Not lost in the misconception of the black man's place
Real…
Ture…
Down…
…and woke!

The complexities and ambiguities of my ambitious mind
      The depth of my spiritualism
      I will touch souls
      Lead the misguided
      Deep-rooted Black…ism
      No estheticism
      You understand my queen…ism
      My word is always bond

Stop questioning my blackness!
      Not ghetto fabulous
      Survival of the smartest
      Bye to the fittest
      Sharpest
      Quick mind
      Tricky
      Sticky
      No mickey's

Are you questioning my blackness because of your insecurity of you
questioning yours?

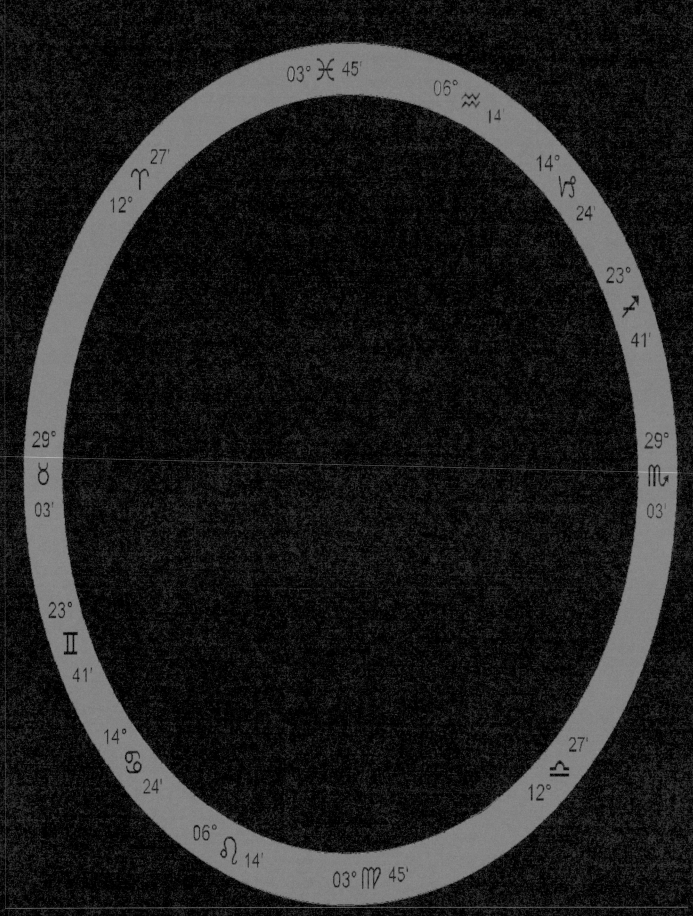

Chapter 5
Zodiac Poetry

Looking to the stars for personality characteristics is an entertaining way to gain insight into a person's character. Today, many of us look to the stars for answers to questions about the compatibility of our relationships. This is my take on the subject… There are four elements: air, water, earth, and fire; each sign falls under one of them.

Fire signs:

Aries
March 21 to April 19

Leo
July 23 to August 22

Sagittarius
November 22 to December 21

Air signs:

Libra
September 23 to October 22

Aquarius
January 20 to February 18

Gemini
May 21 to June 20

Water signs:

Cancer
June 21 to July 22

Scorpio
October 23 to November 21

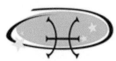

Pisces
February 19 to March 20

Earth signs:

Capricorn
December 22 to January 19

Taurus
April 20 to May 20

Virgo
August 23 to September 22

Rudiments of Fire

We are the inferno heat to passion
With an unpredictable personality
Impulsive spirit
The center of everyone's attention
Aggressive
Quick tempered
Self-confident
Driven

Rudiments of Fire
Leo, Sagittarius, and Aries
Feel our dominating presence
Independent and innovative
      Leo conveys fire's ability to adapt to life's trials and tribulations
Optimistic and passionate
      Sagittarius exposes the power of a fiery love affair
Persistent and courageous
      Aries imitates fire's spawning abilities

The lion's kingdom
I will control my destiny
Feel my rhythmic aura
My confidence will charm you
Impetuous with a vigorous imagination
For I am Leo, let the entertainment begin

The Archer is always ready for action
Energetically spirited
Fulfilling my needs …a must
I see everything
Flexibility you can trust
Change and variety for lust

The out-of-control Ram with a passion for power
Spontaneous adventures keep me focused
Attracted to challenges
Boredom irritates me
Praise my abrasive ego
Never keep me waiting
I am EVERYTHING!

We are the leaders you seek
You will be enthusiastic to meet
We are never indiscreet
Think you can handle the elements of fire?

Down to Earth

We have a discontented temperament
Self-improvement is our self-expression
Materialistically driven
Predictability is our weakness
The same
No change
Defeated by our own insecurities

We are down to Earth
Taurus, Virgo, and Capricorn
The self-reliant and sensual
      Taurus builds on what is existing, a never-changing Earth
Ambitious and proud
      Capricorn posses the authority & power to ground & revolutionize Earth
Frugal and obsessive
      Virgo delivers the strength of the Earth's everlasting music to the motion of change

The benevolent Bull
A bedroom dweller
Financially comfortable
Secretly insatiable
I have everything
Honesty is the key if you want to be with me

The purity of a Virgin
Obsessive perfectionist consumes me
Analytical with an emphasis on anal
Unsolicited advice you should be happy to receive
Virgo's neurotic temperament will seem rude
My sexuality is not service-oriented because I am a prude

The moneymaking Goat
I have a manic ambitious personality
Love brings vulnerability that I can use to benefit me
Accumulating cash proves my masculinity
Capricorn is an achievement seeker
Stability and structure are the ultimate gifts from me to my mate
To lure a Capricorn for love, be prepared to wait

Being down to Earth
We are the practical
Money is our security
Only apply if you are inclined to be grounded

Adaptable Air

We will mentally stimulate your mind
Hypnotic lovers
Communicatively outwit the weaker elements
Positive temperament
Freedom is our spirit
Intriguing to the eye

Timeless air
Gemini, Libra, and Aquarius
Witty and mobile
     Gemini rises above the forces of mutable air
Well-balanced and harmonizing
     Libra regulates the spirit of a light summer breeze
Humane and communicative
     Aquarius embodies the unpredictable fixed air

The unpredictable twins
Thinkers of the universe
Adaptable to all worlds
Challenge my mind
Manipulating public perception
Experimental eccentricity captivates me
The Gemini's mental seduction mesmerizing
Sophistication will optimize all opportunities that strike our interest

Balanced scales
Indulge in our wickedness
I am on an ever-ending journey to find the perfect mate
Love being in love
My passiveness I admit I hate
Harmony and balance keep us grounded
Always keeping peace in my surroundings
Vibrant Libra's indiscretions are filled with passion

The Water Bearer of uniqueness
The true meaning of life
I know everything
Merging of the mind
Escapades delight me
Mind stimulation keeps me occupied
Tie me down and I will disappear
Detached Aquarius will passionately and affectionately entice your mind

Tantalizing
Stimulating
Imaginative freedom riders
Who will teach you things you never knew existed
Total satisfaction fighters
You will never have a dull moment once you recognize
You will be energized by eternal air

Water is My Safe Haven

We are impressionable with an apathetic temperament
Living in confusion
Overly sensitive
Reacting from emotions

My safe haven
Cancer, Scorpio, and Pisces
Emotional and stubborn
      Cancer expresses unpredictable stillness, calmness, forcefulness and abruptness of water
Jealous and horny
      Scorpio conveys the solidification of water
Compassionate and elusive
      Pisces reputation flows between sublimation and deposition of ice

The feel of the Crab
Love closeness
The Yin looking for the Yang
Causing confusion and anarchy
Emotionally draining your psyche
Sexually mimicking a porn star

Do wrong by me and feel my poisonous stinger pierce your flesh
Dominant Scorpion desires love
Vengeful spirit
Addictive personality when my heart is won
Vigilante actions to jealously
Money driven for success
Erogenous Libido for the ultimate test

I am Pisces
Up stream, down stream
I do believe
Nonconforming fishes swimming
A mystery to all
Grammy award-winning performances
You will never know my inner being
Keep everything a secret and I will blow your mind

We are surrounded by water
The three S's
Sensitive soul seekers
Secretive livelihood like a CIA spy
Sexually captivating
Only the strong will survive the wrath of water

Epilogue

Spirituality is the foundation for all thoughts expressed in the previous chapters. Spirituality is the bond that ties all things together.

He is in me

My Lord…
      Let your vision be seen through me
      Allow them to hear your voice through my words
      Let them experience you through me
      Use my physical being to convey your message for those
      You say are in need
Keeping thy faith in the Lord
Showing love and hope is real
My mind, body, and soul are surreal
Holy Ghost in my heart
Holy Trinity embedded within my essence
Praise him
Honor him
Rejoice in the glory of the Divine Almighty
Forgive those who do wrong
Help them see the truth of Jesus Christ our savior
Ask and you shall receive
      Love, hope, and faith
Positivity surrounds such aura that denies negativity
Praise him
Honor him
God uplifts spirituality
When I am…
      Hurt…
            He heals me
      Confused…
            He gives me clarity
      Depressed…
            He uplifts me
      Lost…
            He guides me to the truth
When I need help…
      He talks to me
When I need a shoulder to cry on…
      He consoles me
For he is REAL
He is in me

Author Biography

Expressions from a Reflective Soul is the first book written by Dr. Kimberley Stokes. Dr. Kim, who has been writing for over 20 years, has a doctorate degree in organizational leadership from Argosy University in Denver, CO.

From empty feelings to a new beginning, this book has it all. Dr. Kim goes straight to the heart of relationships, feelings, love, families, and the everyday trials and tribulations of life. She captures the essence of a variety of soulful emotions. This book speaks about …the insecurities, vulnerabilities, and weakness we don't want to admit to. Using the powerful words of poetry, Dr. Kim expresses the manifestation of love and describes how one can create a new beginning.

Expressions from a Reflective Soul will have you questioning some of your answers instead of looking for answers to all of your questions.

Dr. Kim describes her poetry as expressive and to the point. She says, "By experiencing life's ups and downs and listening to other people's trials and tribulations; I have learned that often people are not able to explain how they really feel because they cannot find the right words or sentences to convey it to others. I have been blessed with the ability to articulate those words and sentences to describe the feelings most of us experience."

Dr. Kim who is a native of Newark, New Jersey, grew up in Denver, Colorado and currently resides in Atlanta, Georgia with her husband and sons.

Artist Biography

Floyd Kerr

Floyd Kerr, a native of South Bend, Indiana, has traveled extensively while pursuing a multi-faceted career as an athletic administrator, educator, coach, private investigator, and artist. His travels took him throughout the United States and overseas and served to influence the post-modern, hip-hop, surreal expressionist style of his art. His style is the manifestation of his many cultural experiences, relationships and fond memories of our post-modern world. Many of the works in the book are landscapes on canvas. According to Kerr, the works are "inspired by spiritual experiences from Biblical references to human interaction with a vast cross-section of cultures". One example of this is a piece he calls "Psalms", done in oil on canvas. Kerr says, "This work captures a point in time where I came close to God and walked the path HE placed before me."

Ezra Lamond Stokes

Ezra Stokes, a native of Savannah, GA, started his exploration into the art world at a young age. As quoted by the artist, "Artistry is learned… art is a genetic ability that people are born with." In 2003, Ezra introduced his unique style of art to the world at the Southern University Museum of Art, Baton Rouge, LA. Partnered with his then fiancé (Kimberley Kerr), the couple dazzled viewers with the beautiful combination of visual and verbal art called "Say what I see while I see what you say." Ezra and Kimberley Stokes have four children and reside in Atlanta, GA

Printed in the United States
By Bookmasters